D1299941

The **Depression** and **Bipolar Disorder** Update

Titles in the DISEASE UPDATE series:

DISEASE UPDATE

The **Depression** and **Bipolar Disorder** Update

Alvin and Virginia Silverstein and Laura Silverstein Nunn

Enslow Publishers, Inc.
40 Industrial Road
Box 398
Berkeley Heights, NJ 07922
USA

http://www.enslow.com

Acknowledgments

The authors thank Arman Danielyan, M.D., Ph.D., Research Associate, Department of Child & Adolescent Psychiatry, Cincinnati Children's Hospital Medical Center, and Irene S. Levine, Ph.D., Professor of Psychiatry, NYU School of Medicine, for their careful reading of the manuscript and their many helpful comments and suggestions.

Library of Congress Cataloging-in-Publication Data:

Silverstein, Alvin.
    The depression and bipolar disorder update / Alvin and Virginia Silverstein
and Laura Silverstein Nunn.
       p. cm.— (Disease update)
    Summary: "An introduction to the history and most up-to-date research and treatment of depression and bipolar disorder"—Provided by publisher.
    Includes bibliographical references and index.
    ISBN-13: 978-0-7660-2801-2
    ISBN-10: 0-7660-2801-1
    1. Depression, Mental—Juvenile literature. 2. Manic-depressive illness—Juvenile literature.
  I. Silverstein, Virginia B. II. Nunn, Laura Silverstein. III. Title.
    RC537.S5363 2008
    616.89'5—dc22   2007013854

Printed in the United States of America

10 9 8 7 6 5 4 3 2 1

To Our Readers: We have done our best to make sure all Internet addresses in this book were active and appropriate when we went to press. However, the author and the publisher have no control over and assume no liability for the material available on those Internet sites or on other Web sites they may link to. Any comments or suggestions can be sent by e-mail to comments@enslow.com or to the address on the back cover.

Every effort has been made to locate all copyright holders of material used in this book. If any errors or omissions have occurred, corrections will be made in future editions of this book.

♻ Enslow Publishers, Inc., is committed to printing our books on recycled paper. The paper in every book contains 10% to 30% post-consumer waste (PCW). The cover board on the outside of each book contains 100% PCW. Our goal is to do our part to help young people and the environment too!

Photo credits: © 2007 Jupiterimages Corporation, pp. 35, 41, 52, 76; Associated Press, pp. 47 (Carrey, Cox-Arquette), 104; Courtesy Dr. Lynn Caesar, p. 91; Courtesy Mental Health America of Summit County, p. 31; Enslow Publishers, Inc., pp. 19, 109 (*Melancholia I*); The Image Works: © Bob Daemmrich, p. 63, © Robin Weiner/WirePix, p. 56, © Roger Viollet, pp. 47 (van Gogh), 51; Imagno/Getty Images, pp. 24, 109 (Freud); Library of Congress Prints and Photographs Division, pp. 17, 47 (Lincoln); LifeArt image copyright 1998 Lippincott Williams & Wilkins. All rights reserved, p. 5; © Mark Peterson/Corbis, p. 99; Newscom: Feature Photo Service, p. 82, PR Newswire Photo Service, p. 86; Photo Researchers: John Bavosi, p. 42, Kenneth Murray, p. 27; © Scientifica/Visuals Unlimited, pp. 14, 72; Shutterstock, pp. 10, 53, 58, 89; Tanyth Berkeley for the *New York Times*, p. 94; Wellcome Library, London, p. 21.

Cover photo: Shutterstock (top); Alfred Pasieka / Photo Researchers, Inc. (bottom).

Disclaimer: While the stories of people affected by depression and bipolar disorder in this book are real, many of the names have been changed.

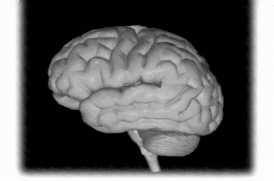

Contents

Depression

What is it?

Depression is a mental disorder characterized by ongoing feelings of sadness, hopelessness, and irritability. It comes in various forms, each of which ranges from mild to severe.

Who gets it?

People of all ages, all ethnic groups, and all genders. It is more commonly identified in adults but often starts in adolescence. Women are diagnosed nearly twice as often as men. However, that difference may be partly due to the fact that men are less likely to seek help.

How do you get it?

People may inherit a tendency to develop depression. Episodes of depression may be triggered by stressful life events, such as the loss of a loved one.

What are the symptoms?

Feelings of sadness, helplessness, hopelessness, and irritability; change of appetite; change in sleeping patterns; loss of interest and pleasure; fatigue; feelings of worthlessness and guilt; difficulty concentrating; thoughts of death or suicide; disturbed thought patterns; and physical symptoms including headache, backache, and stomachache. (A person may not experience all of these symptoms.)

How is it treated?

With medication and psychological therapy.

How can it be prevented?

There is no way to prevent depression. However, learning ways to reduce and handle life's stresses can help to ease symptoms. Getting enough sleep, exercising regularly, and eating a healthy diet may also be helpful.

Bipolar Disorder

What is it?
Bipolar disorder is a mental disorder with periods of depression alternating with periods of extreme "highs" (mania).

Who gets it?
People of all ages, all ethnic groups, and both genders. It is more common among late adolescents and adults. It affects men and women about equally.

How do you get it?
People inherit a tendency to develop the disorder.

What are the symptoms?
Manic mood: overly good mood, increased energy and restlessness, extreme irritability,

racing thoughts and fast talking, inability to concentrate well, little need for sleep, unrealistic ideas and plans, poor judgment, aggressive behavior, and sometimes increased creativity.

Depressed mood: feelings of sadness, helplessness, hopelessness, irritability, and other typical symptoms of depression.

How is it treated?
With medication and psychological therapy.

How can it be prevented?
There is no way to prevent bipolar disorder. However, learning ways to reduce and handle life's stresses can help to ease symptoms. Getting enough sleep, exercising regularly, and eating a healthy diet may also be helpful.

Everyone feels sad sometimes, but clinical depression is serious enough to require medical help. About 3 to 5 percent of people with clinical depression are teenagers.

1

A Matter of Moods

WHEN SHE WAS A CHILD, Maria Stewart often felt sad and lonely. Nearly every day, she was teased by kids at her school. Her home life was not much better. She did not get along with her mother. They could hardly be in the same room without arguing. But Maria did have one person she could turn to when she was feeling down: her grandmother. Her grandmother meant the world to her. Then in 1996, when Maria was thirteen years old, she felt like her world was coming apart. Just a few weeks before Maria started high school, her grandmother died of cancer.

"It destroyed me," Maria remembers. Not long after her grandmother's death, two of her uncles died. "I

> People often use the word *depressed* to describe when they are feeling really sad. But *clinical depression* is more serious than a sad feeling. It is a mood disorder serious enough to need medical help.

wanted to crawl under a rock. I went from a B student to an F student. I lost weight. I kept trying to hurt myself. I didn't see any point in living anymore."[1] Maria's feelings of sadness and frustration continued through high school. In her junior year, a teacher at her school committed suicide. That was the breaking point for Maria. She knew she had to talk to somebody about her feelings. She went to the dean of students, who was a psychiatrist.

Maria told the dean about her symptoms and the upsetting events that had happened in her life. After a long discussion, Maria was diagnosed with clinical depression. She was prescribed antidepressant medication to help her symptoms. She also started individual therapy and family counseling. In therapy, she learned how to talk about her feelings openly and communicate better. She also learned to set goals. Soon she started to do better at school. Her grades improved. She got along with people better and made new friends. She was able to talk to her mother without arguing. She felt like she finally had control over her life.

When Maria went to college, she knew she wanted to help other people. She decided to study to be a teacher for the deaf. "I want to save others from feeling like I did—all alone in the world," she said.[2]

Everyone feels sad or upset at one time or another. You probably have had your share of bad days. That's normal. You may feel sad because of things that happen in your life: You move to a new home and have to make new friends, you have a huge argument with your mom, or someone you love dies. Things like these can make a

What Is a Mood?

When people say they are "in a bad mood," they mean that they are feeling sad, angry, or generally negative. When they are "in a good mood," they are happy, hopeful, and generally positive. Moods can change from day to day or even moment to moment. But eventually they come back to "normal"—that is, the usual mood, or feelings, of a particular person.

In mood disorders, a person's feelings may become too strong and long-lasting. They get in the way of living a normal life. Clinical depression is a common mood disorder that affects millions of people.

person feel very sad. People often use the word *depressed* to describe when they are feeling really sad. But *clinical depression* is more serious than a sad feeling. It is a mood disorder serious enough to need medical help.

Bad moods usually do not last very long. Most people feel better after some time goes by, or after getting a good night's sleep. But people who are clinically depressed have symptoms so overwhelming that they may be unable to handle everyday activities. They feel sad all the time. They have no energy to do anything,

People who are clinically depressed may not have enough energy to get out of bed.

even to get out of bed. They may develop physical symptoms, such as headaches or stomachaches. Depression can cause problems in many areas of a person's life: school, work, and relationships with family members and friends.

Various forms of depression are fairly common. They affect mostly people eighteen and older, but chil-

> **More than 19 million Americans suffer from depression in any given year.**

dren and adolescents can have mood disorders, too. More than 19 million Americans suffer from depression in any given year. About 3 to 5 percent of them are teenagers. That means in a high school class of twenty-five students, depression is likely to strike at least one of them.[3]

Millions of people go undiagnosed because they do not realize that what they have is a medical condition. They do not need to suffer. Mood disorders can be treated. Many people are helped by medication. Psychotherapy, or "talk therapy," is also very important in the treatment process. Getting help can allow people to learn to feel good about themselves and regain control in their lives.

2

Depression
in History

ABRAHAM LINCOLN is considered one of the greatest leaders in American history. He is still admired for his combination of honesty, common sense, and humor. As president of the United States, he had to make important decisions every day. But Lincoln also had a dark side. He was actually a very moody person who suffered from both mild and severe bouts of depression.

Growing up, Lincoln had a difficult home life. During his early years, his mother seemed to be in a constant state of sadness. She died when Abraham was only nine. Young Abe found no comfort from his father. They did not get along and argued constantly. Despite these difficulties, Abraham was not depressed in his

President Abraham Lincoln suffered from depression.

teens and early twenties. In fact, he was very outgoing. People loved to listen to his jokes and stories.

Abraham Lincoln's depression is thought to have started in his mid-twenties, when his good friend Ann Rutledge died in 1835. At one point Lincoln talked about killing himself. His friends and neighbors became so worried about his mental state that they watched over him and did not allow him to have any knives or other dangerous objects.

A few years later, Lincoln began a stormy relationship with his new love, Mary Todd. In January of 1841, Lincoln broke off their engagement. This decision caused him great pain, and he fell deeper into depression. In a letter to a friend, Lincoln wrote, "I am now the most miserable man living."[1] Abraham Lincoln and Mary Todd did get married, in 1842. Even on his wedding day, Lincoln remained depressed, with suicidal thoughts and feelings of worthlessness.[2]

Age-Old Melancholia

Depression is a condition that has been around for thousands of years. Around 400 B.C., Greek physician Hippocrates described depression and called it melancholia (from Greek words meaning "black bile"). This ancient word was used to separate normal sad feelings from those related to what is now called clinical depression. Hippocrates believed that the body held a balance of four main substances called humors: phlegm, blood, yellow bile, and black bile. He believed that a person's basic personality was based on an imbalance of these humors. Too much phlegm in the body made a person calm and unemotional. Too much blood made a person sanguine—cheerful and full of energy. Too much yellow bile made a person choleric—angry and hot-tempered.

Picturing Depression

Picture a sad-looking woman sitting in a courtyard filled with scattered tools, staring blankly into space. This is the subject of a famous engraving by German artist Albrect Dürer. He called his work *Melancholia I*. This masterpiece, completed in 1514, is filled with symbols of doom that reflect the feeling of depression, such as a starving dog and a sad-looking cupid. During the 1500s, a number of other artists created works illustrating images of melancholy.

Melancholia I

Too much black bile caused melancholia—sadness and depression.

In 1621, Robert Burton, an English scholar and clergyman, published *Anatomy of Melancholy*, a book on depression. He wrote about the kinds of melancholy, causes and symptoms of melancholy, as well as a list of cures (which included living in "good air"). The book was a best seller in its time and went through several revised editions in the thirty years that followed.

Seasonal Sadness

Hippocrates also described a kind of depression that was related to the change of seasons. He noticed that people would become sad during the winter when there was less sunlight because of the shortened days. Since Hippocrates' time, this mood disorder has been rediscovered several times. In the 1800s, for example, psychiatrist Jean-Étienne Esquirol was said to be the first to identify this seasonal disorder. However, it was not officially recognized as a mood disorder until the early 1980s. Dr. Norman E. Rosenthal, a psychiatrist and researcher with the National Institutes of Health, rediscovered the link between the shorter, darker days of winter and seasonal depression. Dr. Rosenthal and

This 1936 brochure advertised the European Vi-Tan unit. It promised to treat "sun-starvation," or seasonal affective disorder (SAD).

his colleagues named the condition seasonal affective disorder (SAD). In 1987, the American Psychiatric Association accepted seasonal affective disorder as a true mental disorder.

Treatment for SAD patients actually dates back to the second century A.D., when Greek and Roman doctors realized that a lack of sunlight was the key to the problem. They treated their patients by directing sunlight toward the patients' eyes. For centuries—well into the 1900s—doctors would advise their SAD patients to travel south for the winter, where winter days have more hours of sunlight. Before World War II (1939–1945), most hospitals were built with a solarium, or sunroom. European doctors treated SAD patients with a "light bath"; the treatment was called heliotherapy. It was named after Helios, the Greek god of the sun. Heliotherapy made a comeback in 1984 when Dr. Rosenthal published his first paper on SAD and used light therapy to treat the disorder.

Manic Depression

In the early 1900s, German psychiatrist Emil Kraepelin described another form of depression called manic depression (now often called bipolar disorder). He studied several hundred patients with this condition. They typically had mood swings that went from periods of wild cheeriness to periods of deep despair. Although there were two parts to this illness, Kraepelin considered it a single disease process. He researched the condition, hoping to uncover the nature of the disease and its causes. Kraepelin carefully examined the brains of his patients who had died. However, he could not find any major differences from the brains of people who did not have this mood disorder. He was also unable to come up with an effective treatment. Other psychiatrists felt that

Kraepelin's results proved that manic depression was a disease of the mind, not the body. Therefore, they felt that psychoanalysis (talk therapy) would be the proper treatment. It was soon realized, however, that psycho-analysis did not work on severely depressed or manic patients.

Early Treatments

Throughout history, people with a mental illness were often ignored or treated rather badly. In ancient Phoenicia, mentally ill people were boarded on ships known as the ships of fools. They sailed out to sea to find another place that would care for them. In the Middle Ages, exorcists were used to remove the "demons" from the bodies of those who acted strangely. In the eighteenth century, shock treatments were given to patients by twirling them on stools until they bled from their ears, and then dropping them through trapdoors into icy lakes. Other eigh-teenth-century doctors wrapped electric eels around

In the eighteenth century, shock treatments were given to patients by twirling them on stools until they bled from their ears, and then dropping them through trapdoors into icy lakes.

Sigmund Freud was an Austrian physician who revolutionized ideas about how the human mind works.

their patients' heads as a form of electric shock therapy to treat depression.

In the late 1800s and early 1900s, a lack of effective treatment caused doctors to keep severely mentally ill patients locked up in institutions without any hope of recovery. Around the same time, Austrian physician Sigmund Freud had his own theories about mental illness and how it should be treated. He believed that mental disorders were caused by traumatic childhood experiences. His theories led to the development of psychoanalysis and other psychological methods of treatment.

In 1938, two Italian psychiatrists, Ugo Cerletti and Lucio Bini, used electricity produced by a machine to treat a man with schizophrenia. The electrical shocks were sent through his brain, causing seizures. Earlier studies had shown that these seizures would help lessen the symptoms of mental illness. After several shock therapy sessions, the man's condition greatly improved. This discovery led to the use of shock therapy for patients with other mental disorders, including depression.

Shock therapy was the focus of a novel by Mary Jane Ward, *The Snake Pit*,

Shock therapy is still used today, when other treatment methods have failed. The method has been greatly improved; it is safer and less frightening.

published in 1947. The book painted a horrifying picture from the viewpoint of the heroine, Virginia Cunningham, who was hospitalized after suffering a nervous breakdown. When *The Snake Pit* was made into a movie the following year, shock therapy became a hot topic of conversation. This resulted in a public debate over the safety of this therapy. Nonetheless, shock therapy became the most widely used treatment for serious depression into the 1950s.

Shock therapy is still used today. (Medical experts call it electroconvulsive therapy, or ECT). The method has been greatly improved, and made safer and less frightening. Now doctors use ECT mainly for severely depressed patients and those with certain other mental disorders. It can be useful when other methods have failed.

Discovering Mood Drugs

Almost two thousand years ago, the physician Soranus of Ephesus treated patients with depression and manic depression by having them drink mineral water. About 1800 years ago, the Greek physician Galen treated mania by having his patients bathe in mineral springs and by having them drink from the waters. In the nineteenth and twentieth centuries, mineral baths and spas became very popular in Europe and America because of their healing powers. People who were suffering from nervous breakdowns were sent there for mineral-water treatment.

Until 1949 no one knew what active ingredient in the mineral waters was responsible for their helpful

Mineral springs, like this one in Turkey, have long been used for
natural healing.

effects. An Australian psychiatrist, John Cade, solved the mystery by accident. Cade was analyzing the urine of his manic patients. He was hoping to find a poison that was causing the abnormal behavior. He thought that this poison would be similar to uric acid, a normal chemical in urine. Cade decided to test uric acid on experimental animals to see if it made them manic. He needed a form that dissolved easily in water. He chose lithium urate, a

In 1970, lithium was approved by the Food and Drug Administration (FDA) for the treatment of manic depression. After the patient's mood becomes normal, the treatment is continued to prevent the manic-depression cycles from beginning again.

salt of the metal lithium. (Lithium salts are chemically very similar to table salt.) When Cade gave a lithium urate solution to guinea pigs, he noticed that they became very sluggish.

Cade then tried this chemical on his manic patients, and the results were amazing. Most of his patients responded positively to the treatment. They calmed down to a more normal mood. Actually, urate had nothing to do with it. It was the lithium that produced this effect. In 1970, lithium was approved by the Food and Drug Administration (FDA) for the treatment of manic depression. After the patient's mood becomes normal, the treatment is continued to prevent the manic-depression cycles from beginning again.

In the 1950s, researchers found that a drug used to treat tuberculosis, called iproniazid, raised the mood of some patients. This finding was so striking that researchers started to research the mood-changing properties of the drug. They began to search for other antidepressant drugs as well. This led to the wide assortment of antidepressant drugs that are now available to psychiatrists.

3

What Is Depression?

WHEN SHE WAS A CHILD, Claire Frese could not understand why she felt so miserable all the time. No matter how hard she tried, she just could not enjoy life. She thought that if she could try to act normal and be happy, she would be—but it didn't work. She still felt really sad and lonely. Claire was told that even as a baby, she had cried a lot and was very difficult to calm down.

When Claire began sixth grade in junior high, things started to get worse. She had a hard time dealing with any kind of change. Trying to adjust to a new school made her upset and anxious almost all the time. Nearly every night, Claire could not sleep. Most days she cried uncontrollably. Sometimes she got really angry for no

Claire Frese used her experience with clinical depression to make a video and a Web site to help other kids with depression.

apparent reason and threw terrible temper tantrums. Her mind was constantly filled with negative thoughts. She thought nobody liked her. She even hated herself. When she started threatening to kill herself, her parents realized that this was more than her being a typical moody kid. She needed help. Claire's parents took her to the family doctor.

At the doctor's office, Claire described her symptoms and told the doctor how long she had been feeling this way. The doctor also learned that Claire had a family history of mental illness. Her father and a cousin of his had both been diagnosed with schizophrenia. Based on her symptoms and medical history, the doctor diagnosed clinical depression.

The doctor prescribed an antidepressant to treat Claire's depression. It seemed to help, but it had some bad side effects, so she stopped taking it. Then Claire's parents took her to see a pediatric psychiatrist. Claire's doctor prescribed a number of different medications before they finally found the one that worked best for her. She also started talking to a therapist. The sessions were very helpful. Her therapist showed her how to turn her negative thinking into something positive. She also learned techniques that helped her handle stress better. Thanks to medication and therapy, Claire was able to enjoy a fairly normal life.

At thirteen, when her treatment was working, Claire started to notice that some other kids in her school seemed to have the same symptoms she had. She knew how serious depression could be, and these kids were not getting help. With the help of her mother, doctors, teachers, and friends, Claire made a video about adolescent depression, called *Claire's Story*. The video included symptoms of depression, treatments, and living with depression. It also came with a handbook for teachers, parents, and counselors. *Claire's Story* became an important teaching tool. It has been widely used in health classes throughout the United States and Canada.[1]

Feeling Sad

Depression is more than feeling sad or down in the dumps once in a while. Clinical depression is a medical condition that involves feelings of sadness, despair, and hopelessness. These feelings can go on for weeks, months, or even years. Clinical depression affects a person's thoughts, behavior, and mood.

When people get depressed, everything may seem miserable, bleak, and boring. No matter how hard they try, they cannot just "snap out of it." They feel like they have nothing to look forward to. These feelings are so strong that they may affect every aspect of a person's life. People who are depressed can no longer enjoy activities the way they used to. They may become irritable and moody all the time. Relationships with friends and family start to fall

> Clinical depression is a medical condition that involves feelings of sadness, despair, and hopelessness. These feelings can go on for weeks, months, or even years.

apart. Sometimes the symptoms of depression go away on their own, but many people will not get better without treatment by a professional.

Without treatment, depression can become danger-ous. People who are depressed may try to find a "quick fix." They may turn to alcohol or other drugs to make the pain and misery go away. However, these substances do not fix the problem. Instead, they are likely to lead to more problems and make a depressed person feel worse. Drugs can make people do things they wouldn't normally do. People tak-ing drugs might break the law and get into trouble with the police. They might hurt other people, or themselves.

> Unfortunately, suicide is the third leading cause of death for young people ages 15 to 24 in the United States. Many of those who commit suicide suffered from depression.

In the most serious cases, depression can lead to thoughts of death or suicide. Depression is often described as a black cloud that keeps hovering and doesn't go away. Without any hope of getting better, sui-cide may seem like the only answer. Unfortunately, suicide is the third leading cause of death for young people ages 15 to 24 in the United States.[2] Many of

To Be or Not to Be

"To be or not to be, that is the question." In William Shakespeare's famous play, the title character, Hamlet, speaks these words while considering whether he should kill himself. He has become deeply depressed after the murder of his father. Learning that his mother's new husband is the murderer makes his situation seem even more hopeless. Eventually, Hamlet does manage to get out of his depression and works actively to expose his father's killer.

The play *Hamlet* was written in the early sixteenth century, but Shakespeare's vivid picture of depression could fit right into a modern case history of this mood disorder.

those who commit suicide suffered from depression—a problem that could have been treated.

What's Wrong?

People often ask, "What's wrong?" when they see their friends or family acting differently than usual. A change in thoughts, behaviors, and overall mood is typical in people with depression. They may also experience changes in how they feel physically. Here are various ways depression can affect all aspects of a person's life:

Changes in the Body:

- Difficulty sleeping through the night or getting too much sleep.
- Having a big appetite or almost no appetite.
- Having very little energy—unable to get out of bed in the morning and dragging through the day.
- Getting headaches or stomachaches that don't go away.

Changes in Behavior:

- Becoming bored or losing interest in things that used to be enjoyable, such as sports, hobbies, school, and friends.
- Drinking alcohol or using illegal drugs.

- Skipping everyday activities, such as taking a shower, putting on clean clothes, or going to school or work.

Changes in Feelings:

- Feeling sad and empty. Wanting to cry all the time for reasons that are not clear.

- Feeling angry at people for no obvious reason.

- Feeling hopeless and discouraged, with no hope that these sad feelings will ever go away. Being unable to remember what it was like to be happy before the depression started.

- Feeling guilty all the time.

Changes in Thoughts:

- Confused thinking. Inability to concentrate and to make decisions. Difficulty remembering things.

- Negative thoughts about oneself and one's life. Talking about running away. Thinking that medical treatment will not help.

- Thoughts about death and suicide. Believing that death is the only way to stop the painful feelings and thoughts of depression.

Signs and symptoms of depression can vary greatly from person to person. The symptoms may be mild in some people, and more severe in others. Some people may experience more symptoms than others. When a person experiences severe symptoms of depression for at least two weeks, medical experts call it an episode. Some people may have one episode in a lifetime, while others have one episode after another.

Children and adolescents with depression may behave somewhat differently from depressed adults. Depressed children may refuse to go to school, saying that they have a stomachache or headache. They may

> Signs and symptoms of depression can vary greatly from person to person. The symptoms may be mild in some people, and more severe in others.

act "clingy," wanting to stay with a parent all the time. Older children and teenagers may act out, getting into trouble at school. They may be irritable or have a negative attitude toward everything and everybody. Often they feel as though nobody understands them. These may sound like typical teenage behaviors, but they are severe and long-lasting in depressed teens.

What Causes Depression?

What makes some people more likely than others to develop depression? Actually, there is no single cause. Depression is most likely caused by a combination of factors. They may include the following:

Family history. Depression tends to run in families. Researchers have found that some people inherit genes that make them more likely to develop depression. Genes are chemicals inside each cell that carry inherited traits, such as blue eyes or a small nose. They are passed down from generation to generation.

Life events. Life events, such as the death of a parent, the breakup of a relationship, or poor grades in school can bring on depression. People may also become depressed when they are about to make a major change in their lives, such as graduating from school, starting a new job, or getting married.

Negative personality. People who have a low self-esteem and a negative outlook are more likely to become depressed. Living in a negative, stressful, or unhappy home environment can affect a person's self-esteem and lead to depression.

Brain chemicals. Scientists have found that certain chemicals in the brain play an important role in depression. When the levels of these brain chemicals become too high or too low, the chemical imbalance causes symptoms of depression to develop, including sadness, irritability, and lack of energy.

Other mental illnesses. Symptoms of depression may be part of another mental illness, such as schizophrenia. People can also suffer from depression and another mental illness, such as anxiety disorder or an eating disorder, at the same time.

Medical conditions. People with serious or long-lasting health problems may become depressed.

The Brain Connection

Most cases of depression seem to have one main thing in common: a chemical imbalance in the brain. To understand the link between the brain and depression, first you need to learn some basics about the brain.

Each part of your brain has a special job to do. The outermost layer of the brain is called the cerebral cortex. You use it to think, remember, and make decisions. You also use it to understand and form words and to control body movements. The cerebral cortex receives messages from your ears, eyes, nose, taste buds, and skin. It lets you know what is going on in the world around you.

Deeper inside the brain, there is a kind of relay station that contains billions of nerve cells. These nerve cells receive messages from all over your body and send out messages that control body activities. Special chemicals called neurotransmitters help carry these messages from one part of the brain to another. Whenever you do anything, such as react, feel emotions, or think, your nerve cells fire off messages at very high

Tired After Turkey?

Are you ready for a nap after eating a traditional Thanksgiving turkey dinner? For years, people have blamed the turkey for making them feel sleepy. Turkey contains tryptophan, a chemical that the body changes into serotonin. Serotonin is a neurotransmitter that calms people and makes them feel sleepy. Actually, though, tryptophan works best on an empty stomach—so it's probably not the turkey that makes you sleepy after eating a big Thanksgiving meal. You probably feel tired because you are digesting all the turkey, stuffing, mashed potatoes, yams, and pumpkin pie you ate. Right after a big meal, the brain is not getting as much blood as usual. (Some of the blood is going to the digestive organs instead.) So your brain cells aren't getting enough energy, which is why you may feel like taking a snooze.

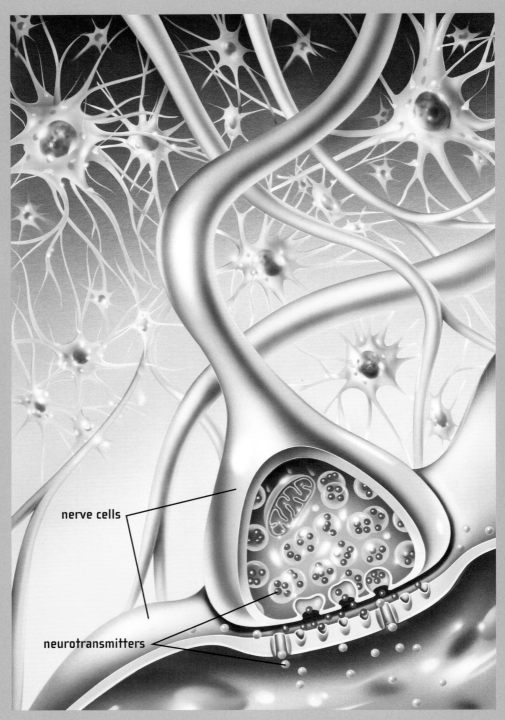

nerve cells

neurotransmitters

Neurotransmitters send signals between nerve cells. They carry messages from one part of the brain to another.

speeds. This fast-paced action makes it possible for you to react quickly to things such as pain. A healthy balance of neurotransmitters helps to keep the different parts of the brain working properly.

Researchers have found a strong link between clinical depression and three neurotransmitters: norepinephrine, serotonin, and dopamine. These chemicals help the nerves to carry messages about happiness, self-esteem, well-being, and other moods and feelings. The brain's message system also lets you know when you are feeling hungry or sleepy. In people with depression, something has gone wrong with the process. There may be too much of one neurotransmitter or not enough of another. This chemical imbalance can cause messages about moods and feelings to get all mixed up, which can lead to symptoms of depression.

4

Types of Depression

WHEN LUISA PEREZ was fourteen years old, she started having periods of sadness that would not go away. She didn't feel like being around anyone anymore. She stopped seeing her friends. She didn't even want to leave the house. Most of the time, she locked herself in her bedroom. She didn't want to do her homework. She didn't want to go to school. Luisa felt as though she had no energy to do anything. Sometimes her sadness was so overwhelming, she thought about killing herself. A number of times Luisa's mother tried to talk to her to find out what was wrong, but their talks often ended in a big argument. Luisa's mother decided that her daughter was probably just being a typical moody teenager.

Luisa's depression continued over the next couple of years. When she was sixteen, her depression finally disappeared. Now instead of feeling sad and tired all the time, she was happy and bursting with energy. She felt as if she could do anything. Her mind was racing with thoughts and ideas. When she talked to people, she often talked so fast her words seemed to blend together. Sometimes people had trouble understanding her. Luisa had so much energy that sleep seemed like a waste of time. She could go for days without sleep and still feel wide awake. She made new friends, but soon she started feeling like her friends were just using her. Luisa figured that they were jealous. "I was the center of the universe," she said later. "I was the chosen one."[1]

Eventually, Luisa's behavior became more extreme. She was having delusions—false beliefs. She started ranting and raving that people were following her. She also told her mom that she had superpowers, that she had the ability to change the colors of objects. By this time, Luisa's mother knew that these moods were anything but normal. Luisa was in the middle of one of her "episodes" when her mother took her to the hospital. At this point, Luisa was a danger to herself—she was thrashing around and tried to jump out of the car.

At the hospital, doctors in the emergency room gave Luisa medicine to calm her down. She stayed in the hospital for two weeks as the doctors watched her shifting moods. In the meantime, they tried out various medications. They also talked to her parents about when all these symptoms began.

> People with major depression have problems eating, sleeping, and thinking. They have negative thoughts about themselves and everything in their lives.

Finally, they sent Luisa home with a therapy plan and a prescription for a combination of drugs. The doctors wanted to wait to see how she responded to treatment before giving her a diagnosis: bipolar disorder.[2]

Bipolar disorder, as described in Luisa's story, is a serious type of depression. This chapter will discuss the various forms that depression can take.

Major Depression

Major depression is the most serious form of clinical depression. People with major depression have little or no control over their lives. Their intense feelings of sadness and hopelessness keep them from functioning normally in their daily lives. (In children and adolescents, the main symptom may be irritability rather than

Some Famous People With Mood Disorders

Name	Occupation	Type of Depression
Terry Bradshaw	Football player, TV football analyst	Major depression
Jim Carrey	Actor	Major depression
Winston Churchill	British politician	Major depression
Kurt Cobain	Singer	Bipolar disorder
Courteney Cox-Arquette	Actress	Postpartum depression
Charles Dickens	Writer	Major depression
DMX (Earl Simmons)	Rapper and actor	Bipolar disorder
Patty Duke	Actress	Bipolar disorder
Carrie Fisher	Actress	Bipolar disorder
Linda Hamilton	Actress	Bipolar disorder
Ernest Hemingway	Writer	Bipolar disorder
Abraham Lincoln	U.S. President	Major depression
Marie Osmond	Singer	Postpartum depression
Brooke Shields	Actress	Postpartum depression
Ludwig van Beethoven	Composer	Bipolar disorder
Vincent van Gogh	Artist	Bipolar disorder
Mike Wallace	TV news anchor	Major depression
Wendy Williams	Olympic diver	Major depression
Virginia Woolf	Writer	Bipolar disorder

a sad mood.) People with major depression have problems eating, sleeping, and thinking. They have negative thoughts about themselves and everything in their lives. In some cases, major depression can lead to suicide.

Dysthymia

Dysthymia is a milder form of clinical depression. It may not stop people from going through their everyday activities the way major depression does, but it does cause a sadness that can last for years at a time. People with dysthymia are not able to fully enjoy good things that happen. Life seems to be "flat" or boring. Other symptoms include low self-esteem, sleep problems, appetite changes, low energy, and feelings of hopelessness. Dysthymia is diagnosed when mild depression has gone on for at least two years. (Children are diagnosed after symptoms have gone on for one year.) In dysthymia, depression may come and go, but the depressed moods are present on most days, for most of the day. People with dysthymia may also have episodes of major depression. This is called "double depression."

Bipolar Disorder

Bipolar disorder, also called manic depression, is a less common but serious mood disorder. It typically develops in people over the age of eighteen. However, Luisa Perez is one of a growing number of people who are showing signs of the illness at a younger age.

Bipolar disorder is identified by alternating periods of highs (mania) and lows (depression). The mood changes can be sudden, but they are usually gradual. During a manic phase, a person may feel happy, excited, overflowing with ideas, and bursting with energy. Later the mood may go crashing down into major depression. The person may find it difficult just to get out of bed and get dressed. Cycles of highs and lows usually follow each other, over months or years.

The depression phase of the disorder has the same symptoms as major depression. The manic phase is very different, however: People may become irritable and distracted. They may feel very happy, like they are on top of the world. They suddenly have lots of energy and become restless. Thoughts are constantly racing through their minds, and they talk really fast. They have a decreased need for sleep. They may act without thinking and show poor judgment. They may have unrealistic beliefs in their abilities and think they have superpowers. They may become suspicious of other people, thinking that they are out to get them. They may abuse alcohol, illegal drugs, and sleeping medication.

Although depression might seem to be the more serious of the two phases, the manic phase can be damaging as well. During the manic phase, a person may stay awake for days or even weeks at a time. The manic person seems to be overflowing with energy, but all the nonstop activity can eventually lead to exhaustion. The person may become sick with an illness that a healthy body could normally have fought off. In addition to the danger of physical illness, the manic person's unrealistic ideas and poor judgment can lead to spending sprees, unplanned pregnancy, or the loss of jobs and friends. A manic episode can wreck a person's life.

> During the manic phase, a person may stay awake for days or even weeks at a time.

Seasonal Affective Disorder

Seasonal affective disorder (SAD) is a type of clinical depression that is linked to the seasons of the year. The most common form of SAD is often called the "winter blues." It occurs only during the fall and winter months, when there is less sunlight because of the shortened

A Creative Link

Scientists believe that there is a link between creativity and manic depression. In fact, studies have indicated that during the manic phase of the disorder, people tend to be more creative than usual. Creative people, such as writers, actors, musicians, and artists, are generally in touch with their feelings and very emotional. They have an ability to see things in a whole different light than the average person. They can express these visions through their writing, acting, music, or paintings.

Self-Portrait with Bandaged Ear, 1889

When creative people become manic, their minds are overflowing with thoughts and ideas, which, in turn, can be used in their works of art.

It is believed that painter Vincent van Gogh suffered from bipolar disorder. His illness was probably responsible for the famous incident in which he cut off his ear after a violent argument with his friend Paul Gauguin. During his manic phase, Van Gogh's bursts of energy often filled him with creative ideas for paintings. Some of his best works were created while he was experiencing a manic phase.

days. The symptoms go away by the spring and summer months. Scientists believe that the lack of sunlight triggers symptoms of clinical depression in people with the winter blues. People with SAD may experience strong feelings of sadness, lack of energy, extreme tired-ness, cravings for sweets and starches, headaches, sleep problems, and irritability.

Summertime Blues

Most people with SAD can't wait for the longer, sunny days of summer. But some people feel depressed during the spring and summer months instead. The cause of these summertime blues is not exactly clear. Researchers think that this rare form of SAD may be caused by a combination of heat, humidity, and possibly the intense, glaring light of summer. In the case of winter blues, treatment involves light therapy, which uses light to relieve symptoms. But for summertime blues, temperature is a factor, not light. There is no effective treatment for this form yet, but some patients have tried cooling devices, such as keeping ice packs handy, to help reduce symptoms.

SAD is most common in people over the age of twenty. It affects about 4 to 6 percent of the population in the United States. SAD seems to be more common in northern regions, where there is less sunlight for many months at a time. For example, studies have shown that SAD is seen in about 10 percent of people living in such northern states as Alaska or New Hampshire. In southern regions, such as Florida, the rate of SAD is only 1 percent.[3]

Postpartum depression affects an estimated 10 to 20 percent of new mothers.

Postpartum Depression

Many new mothers get the "baby blues," usually within the first few days after giving birth. They may go through periods of sadness, irritability, anxiety, and crying. This is all normal for a new mother—especially since she has to deal with physical changes due to hormone changes and extreme tiredness. Giving birth can also be difficult for her emotionally, as she adjusts to her new baby and new responsibilities. Usually these feelings go away within a week. However, some new mothers—an estimated 10 to 20 percent—experience postpartum depression, a condition that is more serious than a case of "baby blues."[4]

Postpartum depression (PPD) is a form of clinical depression. It usually strikes women within the first few months after they give birth, although it can occur within a year. (*Postpartum* is Latin for "after birth.") PPD may cause a new mom to have mood swings, anxiety, guilt, shame, and feelings of sadness that will not go away. She may feel that she is a bad mother. She may even have negative thoughts toward her new baby. The condition can become serious and should be treated right away. Without treatment, PPD can continue for up to two years.

5

Diagnosis and Treatment

AS A TEENAGER, WENDY WILLIAMS was often labeled as "moody" and "overly sensitive." She was uncomfortable talking to people, and she had trouble making friends. When she was fourteen years old, she found a new focus in life: training as a diver for the Olympics. She trained for six hours a day, six days a week while she was in high school. Meanwhile, she could not stop having negative thoughts and feelings of sadness. She even had thoughts of suicide.

In her sophomore year, Wendy went to therapy to learn how to deal with her feelings. Her therapist felt that she was showing signs of depression and suggested she see a psychiatrist, who could prescribe medication.

In 2000, Olympic diver Wendy Williams (far right) teamed with the national campaign Minds in Motion to help raise awareness about depression and encourage people to get help.

Wendy was afraid to take medication and ignored the therapist's advice. Instead, she concentrated on training and winning meets, which helped her put the negative feelings out of her mind. "Focusing on diving kept me going," Wendy said.[1]

When she was twenty-one years old, all of Wendy's hard work paid off. She won a bronze medal for diving in the 1988 summer Olympics. Though her achievement was thrilling, she was already thinking about the next Olympic games. A few months before the start of the 1992 Olympics, however, a spinal injury forced

Wendy to retire from diving. Without diving, there was nothing to keep her from thinking about her problems.

After taking some time off, Wendy decided to move to the island of Maui in Hawaii. She trained to be a massage therapist. For a while, she seemed to be doing well. She was eating a healthy diet and she exercised every day. But then in 1994, her depression came back and gradually got worse. Soon she was feeling miserable all the time. She had no interest in eating and was hardly sleeping. She would stay up all night, and then be exhausted during the day. She had no energy to exercise. In fact, she was too sad to exercise.

"My roommate kept telling me I had to get to the doctor," Wendy recalls. "At the time, I believed that I could overcome it. I'm an athlete. Mind over matter. In one particular horrible moment, I collapsed on the kitchen floor crying, because figuring out what to eat was so overwhelming to me. That's when he put me in the car and took me to a doctor."[2]

Based on Wendy's ongoing symptoms and thoughts of suicide, the doctor diagnosed clinical depression. Right away he prescribed an antidepressant called Zoloft®. At first, she refused to take medication. It took some convincing, but she finally agreed. After only three days of being on the medication, Wendy started to notice a change in her mood. It happened when she and a friend were driving around Maui. She started to notice how beautiful the landscape was. She suddenly realized that this was the first positive thought she had had in a long time. That was only the beginning. Medication turned her life around. She also went to therapy to learn how to turn her negative thoughts into positive ones.

Wendy has since talked publicly about her depression in the media and at conferences for young people.

After starting to take medication, Wendy Williams had her first positive thoughts in a long time while living in Maui.

She wants people to know the importance of treating depression. "The medication saved my life," she explains. "There is no shame in taking it. Depression is a treatable condition. I want to encourage people to get help."[3]

Getting Help

Often friends and family cannot tell the difference between normal sadness and clinical depression. They may tell the depressed person to cheer up, stop moping, or snap out of it. "When you're depressed, you can't snap out of it," explains Helen Egger, a psychiatrist at Duke University Medical Center. "It's something that pervades every aspect of your life."[4] Clearly depression was keeping Wendy Williams from living a normal life. Wendy knew she wasn't feeling right, but like many people with depression, she would not admit she needed help. Fortunately, her roommate could see that something was definitely wrong and made the decision for her. But too often these signs are ignored. If friends and family can learn to recognize the warning signs, they can help the people in their lives get the treatment they need.

Diagnosing depression as early as possible is very important. The longer a person spends in a depressed state, the deeper the depression may grow. Other problems may develop as a result. For example, depressed people may spend a lot of time alone, rather than with friends and family. They may fail to do assigned jobs at school or work. Identifying depression early is especially important for depressed children and teens. They may act out at school or get in trouble with the law. They may also turn to alcohol or illegal drugs in an attempt to feel better.

Suicide

Sometimes people talk to family or friends about wanting to kill themselves. It is their way of asking for help. It should be taken seriously. Too often people think of it as "just talk" and brush it off as though it doesn't mean anything. It is true that not everybody who talks about suicide goes ahead with it, but it is better not to take chances. On the other hand, not everyone who commits suicide talks about it first. Suicide does not happen out of the blue, however. Usually there are signs that have led up to that point. When people learn to recognize these signs, they can provide help.

> Diagnosing depression as early as possible is very important. The longer a person spends in a depressed state, the deeper the depression may grow.

Suicide Risk Factors

Medical experts at Johns Hopkins University have provided a list of typical risk factors and warning signs that may point to suicide:

- ✔ Isolating oneself from family and friends
- ✔ Drastic mood swings or sudden personality changes
- ✔ Neglecting home, finances, or pets
- ✔ An upsetting life event, such as death of a loved one or divorce
- ✔ Constant complaining about aches or pains
- ✔ Giving away prized possessions to loved ones or putting one's affairs in order
- ✔ Sudden calm or cheerfulness after a period of depression
- ✔ Frequent use of alcohol or other drugs
- ✔ Buying a gun
- ✔ Wishing to die or threatening to commit suicide
- ✔ Family history of suicide or previous suicide attempts

It is important to note, however, that not all people who commit suicide show any obvious signs beforehand. And some people who may seem to be suicidal, really are not.[5]

Collecting Information

Where should people go to get help? They can go to their family doctor or to a mental health professional, such as a psychiatrist, to get a proper diagnosis. Unlike many other medical conditions, depression cannot be identified by a blood test, a brain scan, or other laboratory tests. However, these tests, along with a routine physical exam, are important in ruling out physical conditions such as a viral infection or thyroid disorder, which can also cause depression. Usually depression is diagnosed by collecting information about the patient's medical history, as well as that of the patient's family.

The doctor begins by asking the patient for a complete history of symptoms. When did they start? How long do they last? How severe are they? Has the patient had thoughts of death and suicide? The doctor will ask family members about any signs of depression they might have observed. The patient will also be asked about any family history of mood disorders, since depression can be hereditary. Questionnaires that help the patient to identify and describe his or her feelings are also useful. The diagnosis is based on specific guidelines provided by the American Psychiatric Association. Using these guidelines, the doctor can determine the type of mood disorder (major depression, bipolar disorder, SAD, or other) and whether it is mild, moderate, or severe.

A patient's treatment depends on the doctor's evaluation. People with mild depression may do well with

A routine physical exam is an important step in diagnosing clinical depression.

Depression and Mania

Depression and mania can both cause serious problems in a person's life. Below are some warning signs of a possible mood disorder.

Depression	Mania
Feelings of sadness or despair	Feeling on top of the world (extreme happiness)
Feelings of hopelessness; negative outlook	Sudden or extreme irritability or anger
Loss of interest in activities once enjoyed	Unrealistic beliefs in one's abilities
Loss of energy; extreme tiredness	Increased energy, restlessness, racing thoughts, rapid talking
Sleep problems (either too much sleep or not enough)	Less need for sleep
Changes in appetite (either an increase in appetite or a lack of one)	Risky behavior (reckless driving, out-of-control spending sprees, bad business investments)
Problems concentrating, remembering, or making decisions	Poor judgment
Thoughts of death or suicide; suicide attempts	Inappropriate behavior in social situations; suspicion of other people's motives

just psychotherapy. In addition, people with more serious depression may need medication. Many doctors believe that the most effective treatment is a combination of medication and therapy. Researchers who studied 439 adolescents with major depression, for example, reported in 2004 that a combination of Prozac® (fluoxetine) with cognitive-behavioral therapy was more effective than either the drug or therapy alone.[6] Patients need medication to relieve their symptoms, and therapy to learn how to deal with everyday problems, including depression.

Antidepressants

Treatment with medication and therapy can reduce symptoms in 80 to 90 percent of people with depression.[7] The drugs that are used to treat depression are called antidepressants. They are not "happy pills" that magically make a depressed person feel happy. Actually, the purpose of these drugs is to control the chemical balance in the brain. They work by bringing the amounts of brain chemicals—the neurotransmitters—to normal levels.

> Treatment with medication and therapy can reduce symptoms in 80 to 90 percent of people with depression.

As the neurotransmitters reach a healthy balance, symptoms of depression start to disappear.

Treatment is not perfect. What may seem like a "miracle drug" for one person may not work for another. Antidepressants can also have some unpleasant side effects in some people. They may include dry mouth, nausea, headaches, irritability, increased anxiety, dizziness, blurred vision, stomachaches, weight gain, drowsiness, and sleep problems. Usually the side effects go away within a couple of weeks, as the body gets used to the medication. But many people stop treatment too early because the side effects are too unpleasant. (Medication should not be stopped suddenly without talking to the doctor first.)

It may take quite some time to find the right treatment for a particular patient. The doctor may need to adjust the dosage or prescribe different medications until the patient finds something that works. Patients must take their medication every day in order for the treatment to work correctly. It usually takes three to six weeks for an antidepressant drug to become effective. In some people it may take longer, so doctors usually wait eight weeks to decide whether a drug treatment is working. If it is not, the doctor will then prescribe a different drug. When an effective treatment has been found, the medication is usually continued for at least a few months after the depression has lifted. In some cases, the patient may need to take the medication for a longer time, possibly even years.

The National Institute of Mental Health (NIMH) ran a major study of depression treatment on close to 3,000 patients. The results of this study, called the STAR*D study, were reported in 2006. Depressed patients were started on one antidepressant medication. About half either recovered completely or improved. A series of different treatments was tried on those who were not helped by the first drug. The STAR*D study found that patients who responded to the first treatment were most likely to continue to do well. Those who tried two or more different drug treatments were more likely to become depressed again later.[8]

By 2007, there were a number of antidepressants from which to choose. Most of them belong to three main groups, depending on how they work in the brain:

Monoamine oxidase inhibitors (MAOIs) have been around since the early 1950s. Actually, the first antidepressant—the anti-TB drug, iproniazid—was an MAOI. Today MAOIs are not widely used because they can react with certain common foods or medications to produce serious side effects. People who take MAOIs have to avoid foods containing tyramine, a substance found in sausages, beer, red wine, avocados, aged cheese, and smoked fish. MAOIs also should not be combined with most cold and allergy medicines, drugs for diabetes, blood pressure medication, and some pain killers. Side effects can range from headaches and vomiting to a sharp increase in blood pressure and even a risk of bleeding in the brain or death. Despite these problems, MAOIs are still used to treat some people with severe depression. They can be effective when other drugs have not helped.

Tricyclics have also been used since the 1950s. These drugs are most effective for adults and children who suffer from moderate to severe depression. These medications are no longer widely used. Newer antidepressants have fewer side effects. However, tricyclics are still prescribed when other antidepressants have not worked.

Selective serotonin reuptake inhibitors (SSRIs) were the next group of drugs developed to treat depression. Since Prozac® (fluoxetine) and other SSRIs became available in the late 1980s, these drugs have become very popular. In fact, they are often the first drug of choice, mainly because they have fewer side effects than older antidepressants, and the effects are much less severe. SSRIs are commonly used to treat major depression, dysthymia, and seasonal affective disorder.

Researchers have developed other antidepressants as they have learned more about the brain chemicals involved in depression. These newer drugs include serotonin-norepinephrine reuptake inhibitors (SNRIs) and norepinephrine-dopamine reuptake inhibitors (NDRIs).

Treating Bipolar Disorder

While antidepressants work against various forms of depression, they are not usually used to treat bipolar disorder. Lithium carbonate is the drug most commonly prescribed to treat bipolar disorder. This drug, often called just "lithium," is a mood stabilizer—that is, it helps keep the moods in balance. It works mainly to control manic episodes, but it can help to break the whole bipolar cycle and therefore prevent depressive episodes as well. Lithium is also effective in treating mild or moderate episodes of depression that occur as part of the bipolar cycle. Studies have shown that taking lithium can lower the risk of suicide. When depression is very severe, antidepressants may be added. However, doctors are careful in prescribing antidepressants to people with a bipolar disorder because without a mood stabilizer, antidepressants can lead to a manic episode.

Bipolar disorder is a chronic (ongoing) condition. The cycles tend to recur throughout a person's life. Therefore, people must continue to take the medication even when they are feeling "normal." However, they must have regular blood tests while taking lithium. Too much of the drug can cause serious side effects, such as liver, kidney, or thyroid problems.

The Depression Patch

In February 2006, the FDA approved the first skin patch for treating clinical depression in adults. Known as Emsam®, this 24-hour patch works by carrying selegiline, an MAOI drug, through the skin and into the bloodstream. It comes in three doses—6 mg, 9 mg, or 12 mg. At its lowest dose, people can use the drug without the usual MAOI warnings of side effects caused by contact with certain foods and medicines. Steven Galson, director of the FDA's Center for Drug Evaluation and Research, believes that this is a major advance in depression treatment. However, MAOI side effects may occur in people using the higher-dose patches.[9]

Although lithium is the main treatment for bipolar disorder, some patients cannot handle the less serious, but annoying, side effects. These may include extreme thirst, hand tremors (shaking), weight gain, sluggishness, and nausea. Other mood-stabilizing drugs are available for treating manic episodes. The main ones used are Tegretol® (carbamazepine) and Depakote® (valproate). Some drugs that were originally developed

> **Bipolar disorder is a chronic (ongoing) condition. The cycles tend to recur throughout a person's life. Therefore, people must continue to take medication even when they are feeling "normal."**

to treat schizophrenia and other serious mental disorders may also help people with bipolar disorder.

SAD Treatment

People with seasonal affective disorder (SAD) can be treated effectively by using bright artificial light. Light therapy involves specially designed light boxes that produce up to 10,000 lux (twenty times brighter than the amount in the average living room). When people are exposed to this light for at least thirty minutes each day,

A light therapy box can be used to treat seasonal affective disorder (SAD).

after a few days they may experience better mood, better concentration, and more energy. The therapy continues until spring.

Light therapy may produce mild side effects, including nausea, headaches, or eye strain. Usually these problems go away after a while, or when the brightness is reduced.

Some SAD patients are treated with antidepressants, such as SSRIs. Psychotherapy may also be helpful. People with mild symptoms may find it helpful to spend more time outdoors during the day, or to travel south in the winter.

Alternative Treatments

A number of alternative treatments for depression are available without a doctor's prescription. They can be bought over the counter at drugstores and supermarkets as "food supplements." One option is SAMe (pronounced "Sammy;" S-adenosyl-methionine), a natural compound found in body cells. Researchers have found that extra amounts of this substance seem to help a number of conditions, including arthritis (stiff joints), liver disease, memory loss, and mild depression. Studies have shown that SAMe appears to increase the levels of the neurotransmitters serotonin, norepinephrine, and dopamine. SAMe works faster than most antidepressants, and many people can see improvement within two weeks. If there is no change by that time, the dosage may be increased gradually. There are no major side effects. However, people with bipolar disorder should not take SAMe because it can make them manic. Although many people have found SAMe helpful in relieving their depression, the treatment may not work for everyone.

Saint-John's-wort is a plant that has been used for centuries to treat mental disorders and other health conditions. In modern times, this herb has been used to treat depression, anxiety, and sleep disorders. Some studies have shown that Saint-John's-wort works about as well as some antidepressants. However, other studies have found that the herb is not an effective treatment for depression. So does it work or doesn't it? Researchers have concluded that Saint-John's-wort may work for some people and not others, and only in treating *mild* depression.

It is a good idea for a patient to tell the doctor if he or she is taking over-the-counter remedies such as SAMe or Saint-John's-wort, even though they do not require a prescription. These supplements may interact with medication taken for other conditions and cause unpleasant or dangerous side effects. Saint-John's-wort can also make the skin sensitive to sunlight and could result in a bad sunburn.

You may know that fish is good for the heart. But did you know that it is good for the brain, too? Fatty fish, such as salmon, tuna, and sardines, contain large amounts of omega-3 fatty acids. These natural substances not only help reduce the risk of heart disease, but may also lower the risk of depression. Researchers have found that cultures that eat large amounts of fish, such as the Japanese, have the lowest rates of depression. In other studies, it was found that mothers in England who rarely ate fish were twice as likely to develop postpartum depression as those who ate fish regularly.

Scientists believe that omega-3 fatty acids increase serotonin in the brain, giving a similar effect to SSRI antidepressants. In 2002, Dr. Malcolm Peet at Sheffield

> **Researchers have found that cultures that eat large amounts of fish, such as the Japanese, have the lowest rates of depression.**

University in England tested the fish-oil theory. He studied seventy patients with depression, who had not been helped by ongoing drug treatment. After twelve weeks of taking omega-3 fatty acid supplements, 69 percent of the patients showed definite improvement. Researchers say that people can get their dose of omega-3 fatty acids by taking a nutritional supplement

Fatty fish, such as salmon and tuna in sushi, contain omega-3 fatty acids. These acids may lower the risk of heart disease and depression.

or by eating fatty fish (salmon, tuna, or sardines) several times a week. However, there is still some controversy as to whether or not eating fish is effective treatment for depression. Much larger studies are needed.[10]

Talk Therapy

Many medical experts believe that psychotherapy in addition to medication is very important in the treatment of depression. Psychotherapy, or "talk therapy," involves a wide variety of techniques that help people to change their attitudes, emotions, and behavior patterns.

Cognitive therapy is one of the most effective types of therapy for people with depression. The goal is to identify the patient's negative way of thinking and then learn ways to change it into positive thoughts and feelings. This technique is based on the idea that patients who think negatively about themselves and the world will develop feelings of despair and depression. Looking at the positive aspects in his or her life will help the patient develop good self-esteem and a more hopeful outlook.

Interpersonal psychotherapy is a technique that focuses on the patient's personal relationships that led to the depression. The therapist discusses any stresses that might put a strain on relationships. These might include losing a loved one, life changes such as starting a new school or job, or constant fighting between family members or friends. In therapy, patients learn new ways of behaving that would improve their communication skills and relationships with others.

Behavior therapy is based on the idea that depression is a learned behavior. Depressed people have learned to think and behave in destructive ways.

Who's Who?

Psychiatrists? Psychologists? Social workers? Counselors? These are all therapists who can help people with depression, but what are the differences among them?

Psychiatrists are medical doctors. They are the only mental health professionals who can prescribe medications. They can provide talk therapy but usually rely on drugs and other medical treatments for their patients.

Psychologists are not allowed to prescribe medication. They usually have a degree in psychology from a university, rather than a degree from a medical school. Their special training allows them to test and diagnose patients and provide psychological counseling.

Social workers may provide psychological therapy or support for the patient's family. They can connect patients with support groups and get medical and other benefits for them.

Counselors have specialized training in particular areas of mental health. They provide psychological therapy and help patients work through their problems.

Therapy can help them improve their social skills, change how they react to problems, and develop better ways of solving problems. This is a step-by-step process, and behaviors must be identified and tackled one at a time.

Family therapy is a technique that involves bringing the entire family together, with a therapist, to work on specific problems. The goal is to identify the source of trouble in the family, improve communication among all family members, and learn problem-solving skills.

Psychodynamic therapy is based on the same theories as Sigmund Freud's psychoanalysis. The technique involves digging into the person's past to try to uncover troubling childhood experiences that may be responsible for the depression. The therapist helps the person face his or her feelings and learn to deal with them in a useful way. Psychodynamic therapy may be a long process. It is most effective in people with mild to moderate depression.

Shock Therapy

When a patient's depression is so severe that medication and psychotherapy do not seem to help, the doctor may prescribe electroconvulsive therapy (ECT). ECT is also known as electroshock therapy. Small amounts of electricity are sent into the brain, causing seizures. These seizures have been found to relieve symptoms of depression. Years ago, shock therapy was a frightening experience. These days, it is actually a safe, painless procedure. The patient is not awake during the procedure and is closely monitored throughout. However, because of books and movies with frightening images of shock therapy, society still thinks of ECT as a barbaric method of punishment. Actually, ECT can be very effective in treating severely depressed patients. It seems to "reset" the brain chemistry to work in a more balanced manner.

Even though many patients find ECT very effective, it is used only as a last resort. This treatment does have its drawbacks, including memory loss, confusion, disorientation, and anxiety. Although most of these problems clear up within a few hours or days, memory loss may last up to a couple of months or longer.

6

Living With Depression

DURING HIS PROFESSIONAL FOOTBALL career, former Pittsburgh Steelers quarterback Terry Bradshaw seemed to be strong, tough, and indestructible. His strength and determination helped him lead his team to win four Super Bowl championships. Bradshaw retired from football in 1983 and became a television football analyst a year later. He was quickly a hit with audiences, with his strong sense of humor and easygoing personality. In fact, his performance earned him two Emmys for Outstanding Sports Personality.

To most people who met Terry Bradshaw or saw him on TV, he seemed like a happy-go-lucky guy. So it was a surprise when Bradshaw revealed to the public in 2003 that he often had anxiety attacks after games. He explained that his condition got even worse in the late 1990s, after his third divorce. He had gone through bouts of depression before, but that time was different. "I just could not bounce back," he explained. "The anxiety attacks were frequent and extensive. I had weight loss, which I'd never had before. I couldn't stop crying. And if I wasn't crying, I was angry, bitter, hateful, and mean-spirited. I couldn't sleep—couldn't concentrate. It just got crazy."[1]

Former Pittsburgh Steelers quarterback Terry Bradshaw started a campaign to fight the stigma linked to depression.

Bradshaw was diagnosed with clinical depression in 1999. It wasn't easy for him to get help. For a while, he had tried to make the pain go away by drinking alcohol. He drank a lot—so much that he was afraid he was going to drink himself to death. He knew he had to talk to someone about his depression. Finally he went to see his preacher, who started counseling him. Eventually Bradshaw went to a psychiatrist, who told him that he had classic symptoms of depression. He was prescribed an antidepressant, Paxil, and started therapy sessions with the psychiatrist. Bradshaw's life changed dramatically. The drug helped relieve his symptoms, and therapy helped him learn how to deal with his feelings.

In 2003, Bradshaw started a campaign he called his Depression Tour. It involved traveling to a number of U.S. cities in hopes of knocking down the stigma linked to depression. Bradshaw knew what it was like to deal with that stigma. He had been a motivational speaker for many years. Since going public, many companies had asked him not to talk about his mental condition. Even his family didn't want to talk about his depression. In his campaign, Bradshaw wanted to talk openly about his depression and let people know that "it's okay to be depressed. . . . Lots of people are depressed—you're not alone—and I want them to know that if you're clinically depressed there's a solution for you."[2]

After Bradshaw started his public depression tour, he faced a lot of criticism from people in the sports community. By 2006, Bradshaw decided to give up his role as spokesperson for depression. "I got tired of people making fun of me," he said. "I decided, I'm bringing this on myself and I don't need it. There's just idiots out there who refuse to understand what it is—it's a disease. . . . You don't get it from bad food or a needle. It's the way I was made."[3] What Bradshaw learned is that depression still has a strong stigma attached to it. And this stigma prevents many depressed people from getting the help they need.

Still a Stigma

Attitudes toward mental disorders tend to be harsh and uncaring. Many people who suffer from depression are afraid of being labeled as "mental" or "emotionally unstable." Depression is often viewed as a sign of weakness. Men have an especially difficult time admitting that they have problems. Instead of talking to someone, they may turn to alcohol or illegal drugs. This only adds more problems to an already difficult situation. Women are more likely to talk things over with another person. This may be one reason why statistics show that women are more likely to suffer from depression than men. (A woman's depression is more likely to be diagnosed.) And yet, depression is a disease. It should be treated seriously like any other disease. People who have asthma or diabetes are typically given sympathy and support for their diseases. So why should attitudes toward people with depression be any different?

People with mental disorders face discrimination in various aspects of their lives. Applications for insurance policies routinely ask if a person has been treated for mental disorders, and some companies may deny coverage if the answer is yes. People may also have trouble getting certain kinds of jobs if their medical records show treatment for mood disorders. Yet refusing people insurance or jobs based on a history of mental illness is unfair. It is also illegal: The Americans with Disabilities Act (ADA) includes clinical depression and bipolar disorder among the disabilities protected from discrimination in the workplace.

Will people with depression ever be able get the treatment they need without worrying about society judging them? Possibly, someday. But many people still

ROMNEY'S RIGHT TURN TV'S NEW GOLDEN AGE

Newsweek

February 26, 2007 : $4.95

newsweek.msnbc.com

Men and Depression

FOR MILLIONS SUFFERING IN THE
SHADOWS, SCIENCE IS DISCOVERING
NEW WAYS TO DIAGNOSE AND
TREAT A DEBILITATING DISEASE

PHOTOGRAPH BY JOHN MIDGLEY

Men may have a hard time admitting they have depression. Many men suffer silently.

have false beliefs about depression. As it becomes more widely accepted that mental disorders are diseases of the brain that

People with mental disorders face discrimination in various aspects of their lives.

can be diagnosed and treated effectively, then perhaps the ongoing stigmas will gradually disappear.

People with depression often feel as though they are alone—that no one understands what they are going through. Support groups can be very helpful. Being able to talk about symptoms, fears, and treatment decisions with people who *really* understand can be a big help to people living with depression. Some support groups meet in person, but telephone and Internet groups are also available.

Dealing With Stress

Depression makes it very difficult for people to deal with everyday stresses. There are a number of things people can do to get through the day without getting too stressed out.

First, when you are faced with a stressful situation, take a deep breath. Slowly inhale through your nose and then slowly exhale. Deep breathing can actually lower your blood pressure and pulse rate. Using your imagination to create soothing scenery in your mind can also help you to relax.

Exercise is a great way to work off "nervous energy." When the body is active, chemicals called endorphins work in the brain to produce "happy" feelings. Exercise can also make you feel good about yourself, giving you a sense of accomplishment and independence. Studies have shown that exercise is very effective in reducing symptoms of depression. In fact, a study reported in the January 2005 issue of *American Journal of Preventative Medicine* revealed that moderate exercise done for about three hours a week may be as effective as antidepressants in lifting a depressed mood.[4] Some researchers believe that exercise may actually increase the amounts of serotonin and/or norepinephrine in the brain.

> Studies have shown that exercise is very effective in reducing symptoms of depression.

Doing exercises specifically to relax your muscles can also be very helpful. The parts of the body that are under the most stress are the neck, the shoulders, the jaw, and the back.

Eating a healthy diet and not skipping meals can help you to feel your best. Eating properly will keep

Doing an exercise like yoga can help lift a depressed mood.

you from running out of energy during the day. Also, chewing can actually release tension in your jaw muscles. (Chewing gum when you are feeling stressed can help you relax, too.)

Getting a good night's sleep will allow you to feel refreshed when you wake up, ready to tackle the day.

Pets can be good stress-relievers. Studies have shown that pet owners have lower blood pressure than those without pets. Talking to your pets keeps you from thinking about yourself and all of the things you need to do. Stroking your pet can calm your nerves.

Write your problems down in a journal. This can help you to sort them out and make them more manageable and understandable.

Setting aside some time in the day to talk with your family can ease stress. You can tape TV shows to watch when it is more convenient. This will reduce time pressure and allow you to spend some quality time with your family.

Make plans to go out with your friends and see a movie or go shopping. This gives you something to look forward to—and ensures you have company for a while.

Talk to someone about your problems, whether it be a good friend, a family member, or a counselor. Keeping

Spotlight:
Is Laughter the Best Medicine?

Dr. Lynn Caesar (right) laughs with Dr. Madan Kataria (left), the Giggling Guru.

Some people don't agree with the old saying "Laughter is the best medicine." Yet a number of studies have shown that laughter *does* have health benefits, both physical and mental. Dr. Lynn Caesar, a psychologist, believes that there is some truth to these studies. In fact, she has seen firsthand what a difference laughter can make, especially for people with depression.

Dr. Caesar works in Arlington, Massachusetts, as a licensed psychologist and psychotherapist. She is also a certified laughter leader. She earned her laughter certification while attending a workshop in Toronto, Canada, run by Bombay physician Madan Kataria, known as the Giggling Guru. Dr. Caesar was excited about Kataria's ideas of laughter yoga, a program that combines yoga principles with laughter.

In 2004, Dr. Caesar established the Arlington Laughter Club, a program that focuses on laughter as good medicine. In her group, Dr. Caesar uses exercises to encourage people to force a laugh even if there is nothing funny to laugh at. For example, participants may start by telling the group their name and then force out a loud laugh. Every time they have something to say, they finish it off with a laugh. The idea is that getting people to fake laughter will eventually lead to the real thing.[5]

Andy O'Fleish, a participant in Caesar's class, finds that the laughter club really works. He had been depressed for over a year, after he had lost his job. Since joining this program, however, Andy's whole attitude has changed. "It's almost like a high, really. It just picks me up," he said. "I feel like I have a lot of energy for the rest of the day."[6]

your anger and frustrations to yourself can be very unhealthy both emotionally and physically.

Worrying about everything is a waste of energy. Can you control what you're worrying about? If not, then let it go.

Procrastinating can be very stressful. When you put things off, you spend all your time worrying about them. But when the job is done right away, there's no more reason to get all worked up over it.

> Studies have shown that laughter, like exercise, releases endorphins, the body's natural painkillers.

Don't be so hard on yourself if you do not succeed at something. Trying to be perfect can cause a lot of unnecessary stress. Nobody's perfect. Give yourself credit for doing the best you could.

Finally, a great way to handle stress is to have a good sense of humor. Laughter is really the best medicine. In fact, studies have shown that laughter, like exercise, releases endorphins, the body's natural painkillers. A good dose of laughing can have positive effects on a person's mental health, improving memory and alertness, reducing stress, and lifting depression.

Finding ways to avoid stress and learning how to deal with stressful situations are helpful. However, since depression often has a genetic cause, symptoms cannot always be relieved no matter how much the person wants to feel better. Therefore, seeking professional help may be the best solution for those who are clinically depressed.

Deanna Cole-Benjamin suffered from treatment-resistant depression. With the help of deep brain stimulation (DBS), she was able to feel emotions she had not experienced in years.

7

Depression and the Future

DEANNA COLE-BENJAMIN always thought she had a pretty good life. Her childhood was fairly normal. There were no major traumas. At the age of twenty-two, Deanna married a great guy, and later had three healthy children. She was happy living in her nice home in Canada with her wonderful family. But all that changed in 2000. At thirty-six years old, Deanna suddenly felt strange one day. She started having trouble feeling connected to things in her life. "It was like this wall fell around me," she explained. "I felt sadder and sadder and then just numb."[1] Nothing out of the ordinary had happened in her life—there had been no big changes, and no death of a loved one.

Without any warning, Deanna had fallen into a deep depression.

Deanna's doctor prescribed an antidepressant, but it did nothing for her symptoms. She tried drug after drug, but nothing seemed to work, even after the doctor increased the doses. She tried a combination of drugs, but her depression wouldn't budge. Within a couple of months, Deanna was no longer able to do simple every-day things, such as getting out of bed or deciding what to wear. She didn't have the energy to get her children ready for school. She stopped going to work. Everything seemed overwhelming for her.

One day, Deanna went to the doctor's office and told him that she could not handle living anymore. The doctor called her husband, and he came to the office right away. The doctor said that Deanna needed to go to the Kingston Psychiatric Hospital, which was about an hour away. Deanna stayed there for the next ten months, then went for outpatient visits over the follow-ing three years. Her psychiatrist, Dr. Gebrehiwot Abraham, tried nearly every kind of antidepressant, including various combinations of drugs. Deanna also had psychotherapy. In addition, she had nearly a hundred sessions of electroshock therapy—a method that often works for people when all other treatments have failed. But nothing worked. Deanna's situation seemed hopeless.[2]

Switching Off Depression

Deanna is one of millions of people who have what medical experts call treatment-resistant depression (TRD). This condition is so severe that none of the traditional treatments—antidepressants, psychotherapy, and shock therapy—seem to work. Therefore, researchers have been looking for alternative treatments that can bring hope to people with TRD.

In the spring of 2004, Deanna's psychiatrist, Dr. Abraham, was contacted by a research team from the University of Toronto. They were looking for participants in a clinical trial of an experimental surgical treatment for severely depressed people. The method is called deep brain stimulation (DBS). It actually involves two surgical procedures. First, electrodes are inserted in a region near the center of the brain called Area 25. Then a pacemaker device is implanted in the chest, sending tiny amounts of electricity to this "sad center," as it is called. Researchers hoped that this experimental treatment would help severely depressed patients who had not been helped by the usual treatments. Dr. Abraham knew that Deanna would be a good candidate for the trial. Deanna felt she had nothing to lose, so she agreed to have the experimental treatment.

When it came time for the surgery, Deanna had a local anesthetic, but she was awake the whole time. She had to be able to talk to the doctors and answer their questions. One doctor, Dr. Helen Mayberg, told Deanna to let her know if she felt anything different, even if she didn't think it was important. As the doctor probed into her brain, she and Deanna talked now and then. During the beginning of the procedure, Deanna did not mention feeling anything different. Then the device was turned on—without telling Deanna. Suddenly Deanna remarked that for the first time, she felt an emotional connection to the doctor—a feeling she had not experienced in years. Then the stimulator was turned off, again without telling Deanna. Deanna immediately remarked that she must have been mistaken because the feeling had just gone away. The doctors were amazed at the dramatic results. Later, Deanna explained what it felt like: "It was literally like a switch being turned on that had been held down for years. All of a sudden they hit the spot, and I feel so calm and so peaceful. It

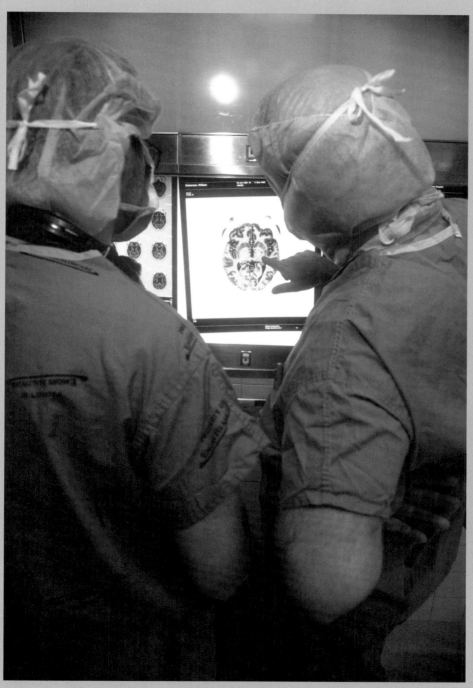

Deep brain stimulation surgeons evaluate a brain scan. DBS could become an important treatment for clinical depression.

was overwhelming to be able to process emotion on somebody's face. I'd been numb to that for so long."[3]

Deanna is not the only success story. Out of twelve patients who participated in the study, eight of them (including Deanna) felt that the treatment lifted their depression. Unlike shock therapy, this treatment produced no negative side effects. The reason for this could be that shock therapy involves 70 to 150 volts of electricity traveling through the entire brain. Deep brain stimulation, however, sends only about 4 volts to a very small area in the brain—about the size of a pea. After treatment, these patients reported being able to live full lives again.

While DBS treatment appears promising, researchers do not know whether or not the results are long-lasting. In addition, the operation is very expensive (about $40,000 in 2007), and it is not covered by insurance because it is experimental. Still, researchers believe that this is a huge advance in research on depression treatment. For severely depressed people, DBS could be a real lifesaver. "This promises to give us the opportunity to rescue people who are hopelessly depressed and on the road to suicide and for whom nothing else has worked," says Dr. Zul Merali, president of the Institute of Mental Health Research in Ottawa.[4]

Magnetic Treatment

Though DBS is a promising approach, it involves surgery. Any surgery—especially brain surgery—involves risk. Therefore, researchers have been looking for safer methods of treatment. One option is called transcranial magnetic stimulation (TMS). TMS does not involve surgery, and the patient can go home the same day.

In TMS, the doctor holds a paddle-shaped device that produces a magnetic field over the patient's forehead. The powerful magnetic field causes nerve cells inside the brain to start working. The nerve cells produce a tiny electric current in the upper front part of the brain. (Usually there is not much activity in this part of the brain when someone is depressed.) The amount of electricity produced in the brain is much smaller than the huge jolt caused by shock therapy. It is much more focused, though, targeting a specific area of the brain. (In shock therapy the whole brain is affected.)

In clinical studies of TMS, many patients with treatment-resistant depression felt somewhat better within a week. Most of the patients were much better

A Surprise Discovery

Like many discoveries, magnetism was found to relieve depression quite by accident. At McLean Hospital near Boston, researchers were trying to find possible new treatments by taking brain scans of thirty people with bipolar disorder. Some of these participants were receiving medication and others were not. After a 45-minute brain scan, the first patient, who had been so depressed she could barely speak, was suddenly bubbling with enthusiasm and talking nonstop. The next patient, who could barely crack a smile, started telling jokes after the brain scan. The following couple of patients had similar experiences.

The technician, Aimee Parow, was surprised at the positive effect the machine had on the participants. She told her boss about her observations—that the patients' depression seemed to be lifted after being exposed to the brain scan's electromagnetism. Together they decided that their study had a new focus: to see if electromagnetism *really* does work in curing major depression. In January 2004, they reported in *American Journal of Psychiatry* that 23 out of 30 people who participated in the study said their depression was greatly improved after the brain scan.[6]

after two weeks of daily twenty-minute treatments. Not only was their mood improved, but they were also able to think and work better. TMS does not cause the memory loss that shock therapy produces. So far the only negative side effect observed after TMS is a mild headache in about 20 percent of the patients.[5] (The headaches quickly go away after treatment with aspirin or acetaminophen.)

Hitting the Right Nerve

In July 2005, the FDA approved the vagus nerve stimulator (VNS) as an alternative treatment for people with treatment-resistant depression. Initially, this device was approved in 1997 for the treatment of epilepsy. Its effects on depression were discovered when epilepsy patients who were also depressed reported that their mood improved after VNS treatment. Since the 2005 FDA approval, people with TRD finally have hope of a long-term treatment option that can be covered by insurance companies.

In July 2005, the FDA approved the vagus nerve stimulator (VNS) as an alternative treatment for people with treatment-resistant depression. Its effects on depression were discovered when epilepsy patients who were also depressed reported that their mood improved after VNS treatment.

In VNS, a pulse generator, somewhat like a pacemaker, is surgically implanted under the skin of the left chest. An electrical wire leading from the device connects to the left vagus nerve in the neck. When the device is turned on, tiny amounts of electricity are sent along the wire from the battery-powered generator to the vagus nerve. The electrical impulses are then sent to the brain. The patient can turn the device off by

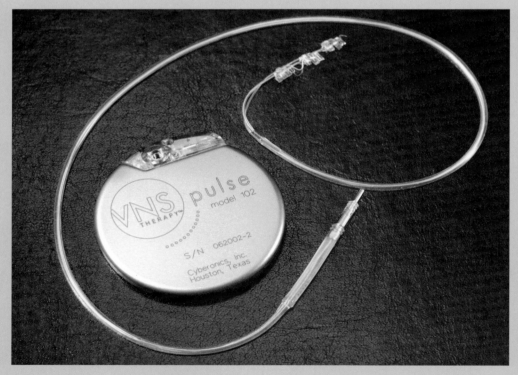

Vagus nerve stimulators are surgically implanted in the body. They help treat depression by sending electrical impulses to the brain and changing the way neurotransmitters carry messages.

holding a magnet over the generator. Researchers have found that VNS changes the way norepinephrine, serotonin, and other brain neurotransmitters carry messages in the brain. Studies have shown that VNS is a safe, effective treatment option. However, it does not work for everyone. In addition, patients may not see results until after three months of therapy.

*   *   *

Since the 1950s, researchers have learned a great deal about clinical depression. This knowledge has led to a wide variety of treatment options that now give people hope of escaping the darkness of depression. Yet the stigma of "mental illness" has kept many people from getting help. Better public education is needed to help erase the stigma. Without the fear of being labeled, more people with depression may be able to seek help and gain control of their lives.

Questions and Answers

My mom says all I ever do is mope around. She keeps telling me to "get over it," but I can't. I just don't feel like doing anything anymore. I can't seem to focus on my homework. I don't even want to go out with my friends. What's wrong with me? Do all teenagers feel this way? The idea that all teenagers are moody and that they'll "get over it" is not necessarily true. Their moodiness could be a sign of clinical depression. Even though most people with depression are adults, teenagers and children can have it, too. Talk to a counselor or a mental health professional to find out for sure.

I heard that a guy on the high school football team has been diagnosed with depression. How can that be? Football players are tough. They can't get depression, can they? Depression is not a sign of weakness. It can affect *anyone*. Too often guys do not get help because they are expected to be strong and keep all their feelings to themselves. That can be dangerous. Depression is the leading cause of suicide.

I have been diagnosed with clinical depression. My parents want me to have psychotherapy. What good will that do? Won't talking about my problems just make me feel worse? It is possible that you may feel bad at first. But a therapist can help you understand your problems better, and why they make you upset. Then you can learn ways to deal with your problems.

My best friend keeps saying things like, "If I died tomorrow, I bet nobody would even notice," and, "My life is worthless." I tried to make her feel better, but she wouldn't listen to me. I don't think she would actually hurt herself, so should I tell anyone? Yes, you definitely should tell a responsible adult—a parent, counselor, or sympathetic teacher. Although some people who say things like that are "just talking," some actually are thinking seriously about suicide. If they don't get help, they may go through with it.

My mom just told me that my dad was diagnosed with bipolar disorder. He had always been really moody. Sometimes, he'd sit in his bedroom and wouldn't come out for hours. He even made my mom call in sick for him a couple of times because he didn't "feel up to going to work." Other times he'd be in a great mood, like he's on top of the world. He also made some bad investments and lost a lot of money. Now I understand why he acted that way. My question is: Am I going to be like that too when I get older? Not necessarily, but you do have a higher risk than the average person because bipolar disorder is hereditary. Just be alert for the warning signs, especially starting in your late teens. Don't make yourself miserable worrying about it, though. Mood disorders are treatable, and getting diagnosed is the first step to getting help.

After reading about seasonal affective disorder (SAD), I realized that every winter I get pretty depressed and I don't have much energy to do anything. By the springtime, though, I start to get "spring fever." I have a ton of energy and I can't wait to play outside. Does that mean that I have SAD? What you described is very common and happens to lots of people. But that doesn't necessarily mean that you suffer from SAD. If you find that the depression is affecting your relationships with family and friends, or it keeps you from doing your normal everyday activities, then it could be SAD. You should see a professional to be certain.

I have been taking antidepressants for almost a week, and I am starting to get really bad side effects. They're making me feel anxious all the time. Will the anxiety go away? I can't stand feeling that way. Can I just stop taking the medicine? A common problem with antidepressants is that they can have very unpleasant side effects. Usually they go away within a couple of weeks, but some people want to stop their medication before then. It is very important to talk to your doctor first, before you stop taking antidepressants. Sometimes adjusting the dose can reduce the side effects. Also, there are many different drugs to choose from. You may have to try a number of them before you find the right medicine for you.

Depression Timeline

400 B.C. ...... Hippocrates describes melancholia (depression).

100s A.D. ...... Soranus of Ephesus treats depression and manic depression with mineral water.

1514 .... Albrecht Dürer completes the engraving *Melancholia I*.

1621 .... Robert Burton publishes *Anatomy of Melancholy*.

mid-1800s .... Jean-Étienne Esquirol notes a link between seasons and some depressions.

1890s .... Sigmund Freud first presents his ideas on psychoanalysis.

early 1900s ...... Emil Kraepelin describes manic depression.

1938 .... Italian psychiatrists Ugo Cerletti and Lucio Bini's shock treatment of a man with schizophrenia leads to the development of shock therapy.

1948 .... The hit movie *The Snake Pit*, based on Mary Jane Ward's novel, stirs up controversy over the safety of shock therapy.

1949	John Cade discovers lithium's effects on manic patients.
1950s	The anti-TB drug iproniazid is found to work against depression.
1951	A patent is given for imipramine, the first tricyclic antidepressant.
1960s	Monoamine oxidase inhibitors are widely used to treat depression.
1970	The FDA approves lithium as a treatment for manic depression.
1984	Norman E. Rosenthal identifies seasonal affective disorder (SAD) and suggests light therapy.
1987	The American Psychiatric Association recognizes SAD as a mental disorder.
1988	The FDA approves Prozac® (fluoxetine) as a treatment for depression.
2005	The FDA approves vagus nerve stimulation (VNS) for treatment-resistant depression.
2006	The FDA approves the first skin patch to treat depression.

For More Information

American Academy of Child and Adolescent Psychiatry
3615 Wisconsin Avenue, N.W.
Washington, DC 20016-3007
Phone: (202) 966-7300
Fax: (202) 966-2891
Web site: www.aacap.org

American Foundation for Suicide Prevention
120 Wall Street, 22nd Floor
New York, NY 10005
E-mail: inquiry@afsp.org
Toll-free: (888) 333-AFSP
Phone: (212) 363-3500
Web site: www.afsp.org

American Psychiatric Association (APA)
1000 Wilson Blvd.
Suite 1825
Arlington, VA 22209
Toll-free: (888) 35-PSYCH
Phone: (703) 907-7300
Web site: www.healthyminds.org

Child and Adolescent Bipolar Foundation
1000 Skokie Blvd., Suite 570
Wilmette, IL 60091
E-mail: cabf@bpkids.org
Phone: (847) 256-8525
Fax: (847) 920-9498
Web site: www.bpkids.org

Depression and Bipolar Support Alliance (DBSA)
730 N. Franklin Street, Suite 501
Chicago, IL 60610-7224
Toll-free: (800) 826-3632
Web site: www.dbsalliance.org

National Alliance for Mental Illness (NAMI)
Colonial Place Three
2107 Wilson Blvd., Suite 300
Arlington, VA 22201-3042
Phone: (703) 524-7600
Information Helpline: (800) 950-NAMI (6264)
Web site: www.nami.org

National Hopeline Network
24-hour Crisis Hotline
Phone: 1-800-SUICIDE (1-800-784-2433)

National Institute of Mental Health (NIMH)
6001 Executive Boulevard, Room 8184, MSC 9663
Bethesda, MD 20892-9663
Toll-free: (866) 615-6464
E-mail: nimhinfo@nih.gov
Web site (general): www.nimh.nih.gov/

National Mental Health Association (NMHA)
2001 N. Beauregard Street, 12th Floor
Alexandria, VA 22311
Toll-free: (800) 969-6642
Hotline: (800) 273-TALK (8255)
Web site: www.nmha.org

Suicide Prevention Action Network USA (SPAN USA)
1025 Vermont Avenue, NW, Suite 1066
Washington, DC 20005
E-mail: info@spanusa.org
Phone: (202) 449-3600
Web site: www.spanusa.org

Chapter Notes

Chapter 1. A Matter of Moods

1. Dianne Hales and Dr. Robert E. Hales, "When a Teenager Is Sad . . . ," *Parade Magazine*, May 5, 2002, p. 4.

2. Ibid.

3. NIMH (National Institute of Mental Health), "What To Do when a Friend Is Depressed," *NIMH Publication No. 01-3824*, February 17, 2006, <http://www.nimh.nih.gov/publicat/friend. cfm> (June 27, 2007).

Chapter 2. Depression in History

1. Joshua Wolf Shenk. *Lincoln's Melancholy* (Boston: Houghton Mifflin), 2005, p. 43.

2. Ibid., pp. 11–43, 95–96; R. J. Norton, "Depressed? Read Abraham Lincoln's Words," *Abraham Lincoln Research Site*, November 28, 2002, <http://home.att.net/~rjnorton/Lincoln84.html> (November 17, 2006).

Chapter 3. What Is Depression?

1. Claire Frese, "Claire's Story," modified March 22, 2005, <http:// www.clairesstory.org/clairesstory.html> (November 1, 2006).

2. National Institute of Mental Health, "In Harm's Way: Suicide in America," updated February 17, 2006, <http://www.nimh.nih.gov/publicat/harmsway.cfm> (November 22, 2006).

Chapter 4. Types of Depression

1. Jeffrey Kluger and Sora Song, "Young and Bipolar," *Time*, August 19, 2002, p. 40.

2. Ibid., pp. 38–51.

3. Josepha Chong, "Seasonal Affective Disorder," *PyschCentral*, October 19, 2006, <http://psychcentral.com/lib/2006/10/seasonal-affective-disorder/> (December 6, 2006).

4. Ricardo J. Fernandez, "Postpartum Depression: Frequently Asked Questions," *State of New Jersey Department of Health and Senior Services*, modified October 20, 2005, <http://www.state.nj.us/health/fhs/ppd/healthcare-faq.shtml> (December 14, 2006).

Chapter 5. Diagnosis and Treatment

1. Sarah Shelton, "Diving solace in battle with illness," *The Journal*, December 10, 2003, <http://www.webujournal.com/media/storage/paper245/news/2003/12/10/Sports/Diving.Solace.In.Battle.With.Illness576223.shtml?norewrite200612141340&sourcedomain=www.webujournal.com> (December 14, 2006).

2. Adele Slaughter, "Wendy Williams dives into depression awareness," *USAToday.com*, August 10, 2001, <http://www.usatoday.com/news/health/spotlight/2001-08-10-williams-depression.htm> (December 14, 2006).

3. Claudia Perry, "A game plan: Female athletes spread the word on getting help for depression," *The Star-Ledger* (Newark, NJ), October 10, 2000, p. 47.

4. Kathiam M. Kowalski, "Dealing with depression—beyond the blues," *Current Health 2*, December 1999, p. 7.

5. Karen L. Swartz, *The Johns Hopkins White Papers: Depression and Anxiety* (Baltimore, MD: Johns Hopkins Medicine), 2006, pp. 16–17.

6. Marilyn Weeks, "Combination Treatment Most Effective in Adolescents with Depression," *National Institute*

of Mental Health, August 17, 2004, <http://www.nimh. nih.gov/press/ prtads.cfm> (April 15, 2007).

7. American Psychiatric Association, "Let's Talk Facts About Depression," © 2005, <http://healthyminds.org/multimedia/ depression.pdf> (November 28, 2006).

8. National Institute of Mental Health, "Odds of Beating Depression Diminish as Additional Treatment Strategies Are Needed," November 1, 2006, <http://www.nimh.gov/press/ stardomnibus.cfm> (April 16, 2007); National Institute of Mental Health, "Questions and Answers about the NIMH Sequenced Treatment Alternatives To Relieve Depression (STAR*D) Study—All Medication Levels," November 2006, <http://www.nimh.nih. gov/healthinformation/stard-qa-overall.cfm> (April 16, 2007).

9. "First Depression Patch Approved," *FDA Consumer*, May–June 2006, p. 4.

10. John McKenzie, "Fish Oil Helps Treat Depression," *ABC News*, August 19, 2006, <http://abcnews.go.com/WNT/ Health/story?id=129498&page=1> (December 27, 2006).

Chapter 6. Living With Depression

1. John Morgan, "Terry Bradshaw's Winning Drive Against Depression," *USAToday.com*, January 30, 2004, <http://www.usatoday.com/news/health/spotlighthealth/ 2004-01-30-bradshaw_x.htm> (December 28, 2006).

2. Ibid.

3. Mark Washburn, "Football Star Scorned Over Depression," *The Charlotte Observer*, September 25, 2006, <http://www.charlotte.com/mld/charlotte/living/health/ 15607519.htm> (October 27, 2006).

4. Kate Murphy, "Easing Depression Without Drugs," *Business Week*, May 2, 2005, p. 94.

5. Phil Primack, "Grin Reaper," *The Boston Globe*, February 6, 2005, <http://www.boston.com/news/globe/magazine/articles/2005/02/06/grin_reaper/> (December 22, 2006).

6. "People in 'Laughter Groups' Giggle and Guffaw for Better Health," *ABC News*, April 30, 2005, <http://abcnews.go.com/GMA/PainManagement/story?id=717261&page=1> (January 2, 2007).

Chapter 7. Depression and the Future

1. David Dobbs, "A Depression Switch?" *New York Times Magazine*, April 2, 2006, p. 50.

2. Ibid., pp. 50–55; Richard Starnes, "Surgery Can Flick Switch on Depression," *The Ottawa Citizen*, April 7, 2006, <http://www.canada.com/ottawa/news/city/story.html?id=5715b26c-4ee6-4a69-8fae-18cba9831c55&k=65134> (January 8, 2007).

3. Dobbs, p. 54.

4. Starnes.

5. Mark S. George, "Transcranial Magnetic Stimulation: Magnets for Depression," *DiscoveryHealth: Alternative Health*, July 12, 2005, <http://health.discovery.com/centers/althealth/tms/ depression.html> (January 11, 2007).

6. Marianne Szegedy-Maszak, "Magnetism and the Brain," *U.S. News and World Report*, February 16, 2004, pp. 53–54.

Glossary

antidepressant drug—Medication used to treat clinical depression by restoring the balance of neurotransmitters.

bipolar disorder—Also known as *manic depression*; a form of mood disorder that involves cycles of extreme happiness (mania) to utter despair (depression).

cerebral cortex—The outermost layer of the brain. We use it to think, remember, make decisions, and control the movements of the body.

chemical imbalance—Having levels of certain neurotransmitters that are too high or too low.

clinical depression—Depression that is long-lasting and/or impairs a person's ability to function normally.

dopamine—A neurotransmitter that helps control attention, motivation, alertness, and the ability to experience pleasure.

dysthymia—A mild form of depression that is long-term, lasting for months or even years at a time; it is diagnosed after going on for at least two years in adults, or one year in children.

electroconvulsive therapy (ECT)—Also known as "shock therapy"; a type of treatment that produces seizures in severely depressed patients to improve their mood.

endorphins—Chemicals released in the brain that carry "happy" messages.

episode—A period of time in which severe symptoms occur. In bipolar disorder, manic episodes may alternate with depressive episodes.

gene—Hereditary material inside body cells that carries information about a person's characteristics.

hormones—Chemicals released into the bloodstream that help to control and regulate the body's activities.

light therapy—A method of treatment for SAD patients in which "light boxes" are used to provide enough light to relieve their depression.

lithium—The most commonly prescribed medication for patients with bipolar disorder.

major depression—The most severe form of depression; patients have little or no control over their lives, making it difficult for them to function normally in everyday activities.

melancholia—A term for severe depression, first coined by ancient Greek physician Hippocrates.

monoamine oxidase inhibitors (MAOIs)—A group of antidepressant drugs, such as Marplan® (isocarboxazid) and Nardil® (phenelzine), usually prescribed only to severely depressed patients.

mood disorder—A mental condition in which emotions become strong and long-lasting, and interfere with normal everyday activities.

neurotransmitter—A chemical that carries messages from one part of the brain to another.

norepinephrine—A neurotransmitter that works in the brain to help provide energy, alertness, and focus attention.

postpartum depression—A form of depression that strikes mothers within several months of giving birth; it causes mood swings, anxiety, guilt, shame, and feelings of sadness that may last for up to two years.

psychotherapy—"Talk therapy"; treatment involving a wide variety of techniques that help people to change their attitudes, emotions, and behavior patterns.

schizophrenia—A severe mental disorder characterized by illogical thinking, hallucinations, and disorganized speech and behavior.

seasonal affective disorder (SAD)—A form of depression that occurs around the same time every year, most commonly during the fall and winter months when there is less sunlight.

seizure—A sudden attack of violent, uncontrollable, muscle movements.

selective serotonin reuptake inhibitors (SSRIs)—
A group of antidepressant drugs that include
Prozac® (fluoxetine).

serotonin—A type of neurotransmitter that is
connected to mood and sleep cycles.

STAR*D—Sequenced Treatment Alternatives to
Relieve Depression; a large study of the effectiveness
of depression treatments.

stigma—Shame or disgrace attached to something
regarded as socially unacceptable.

treatment-resistant depression (TRD)—A severe
type of depression that is not helped by traditional
treatments, including antidepressants, psychotherapy,
and shock therapy.

tricyclic antidepressants—A group of
antidepressant drugs, such as Tofranil® (imipramine)
and Norpramin® (desipramine), named for their
chemical structure, which includes three rings of
carbon atoms.

vagus nerve—One of the twelve pairs of nerves that
connect the brain to other parts of the body.

Further Reading

Mintle, Linda. *Breaking Free From Depression*. Lake Mary, Fla.: Charisma House, 2002.

Roy, Jennifer Rozines. *Depression*. New York: Benchmark Books, 2005.

Scowen, Kate. *My Kind of Sad: What It's Like to Be Young and Depressed*. Toronto, Ontario: Annick Press, 2006.

Smith, Laura L. and Charles H. Elliott. *Anxiety & Depression for Dummies*. Hoboken, N.J.: Wiley Publishing, Inc., 2006.

Zucker, Faye. *Depression*. New York: Franklin Watts, 2003.

Internet Addresses

American Psychiatric Association (APA). Healthy Minds. Healthy Lives. *Psychotherapy.*
<http://healthyminds.org/psychotherapy.cfm>

Depression and Bipolar Support Alliance.
<http://www.dbsalliance.org>

National Institute of Mental Health.
<http://www.nimh.nih.gov/healthinformation/depressionmenu.cfm>

Index